Books by Georgia S. McDade

Travel Tips for Dream Trips
Outside the Cave (two versions)
Outside the Cave II (two versions)
Outside the Cave III
Outside the Cave IV
Observations and Revelations

The Unlevel Field

Poems

by

Georgia S. McDade

The Unlevel Field © 2023 Georgia S. McDade
All rights reserved. No part of this publication may be reproduced or transmitted in any form or by any means, electronic or mechanical, including photocopy, recording, or any information storage or retrieval system now known or to be invented, without permission in writing of the author, except by reviewers who wish to quote brief passages in connection with a review written for publication in print and electronic form.

Cover Art: 'Desert Annuals in Bloom' ⓒ by Jim Morefield, via Flickr
Cover design by Vladimir Verano

Contact the author: gsmcdade@msn.com

ISBN: 978-0-9821872-4-1

Acknowledgements

Thank you, reader. You keep me writing.

Ideas for several of my poems come from artists in various media. Thanks to Thomas Ager, Jasmine Brown, Carol d'inferno, Esther Ervin, and David Traynor whose works inspired me to write some of the poems in this volume.

Thanks to the persons whose words evoked a response, sometimes positive other times negative: Virginia Kruta, Bill O'Reilly, Martin Niemöller, Michelle Obama, Jon Stewart, Mark Thompson, and Jim Wallis; Andrew Hacker; and the 1968 "Report of the National Advisory Commission on Civil Disorders" (Kerner Commission), which unfortunately continues to ring true.

Donald Trump belongs in this group because so often he made a statement or committed a deed that I felt demanded a response. For approximately five years, he more than any other being was responsible for the overflow of my feelings and my failure to recollect in tranquility.

I thank author Sharon Chang who wrote the introduction despite her busy schedule.

I am greatly indebted to Alain Patience Mizero for his technical skills. Had he not helped with the formatting, I would be working on the computer now, and you would not be reading this book!

Great thanks go to Mary Bonine who patiently helped and encouraged me through various phases of the formatting. She was working as I worked on other projects! Thanks to Vladimir Verano for the final touches.

Finally, I am grateful for the internet, the news, and news media, all of which put so much information at my fingertips!

Table of Contents

FOREWORD i

INTERROGATIVES

I Am in a Hurry! 1
My Wants 2
Precarity 3
Where Is He? 4
Thank You, Mr. Trump! 5
What Trump Can't Do 6
The Last Look 9
A Good Catch 10
They Do Not Know What They Do 11
Asking for Help 13
Acceptable? 14
A Chance? 15
Crispus Attucks 16
Whose America? 17
What They Do 18
The Absence of a Presence 19
What's American—Or Not 20
Want to Judge? 21

EXCLAMATIONS

Journeys 25
Reclaiming Time 26
Trapped in an Era 27
A Hog Speaks: Wall Street Humans 28
What Can't and Can Be Imagined 30
The Color of One's Skin 32
Undeserved Guilt 33

Futility of Worry 34
Minds and Marriage 35
Seeing the Light 36
Capital Punishment 36
Not the One 37
Resiliency 38
Thanks, 63,000,000 39
Randomness of the Grim Reaper 40
Morning Greetings 41
An Outsider Speaks 42
Preoccupied with Horror 43
Being 44
Pie Chart of My Life 45
The Day the Pill Went on the Market 46
An Addendum 47
That Look 48
Degrees of Strange 49

IMPERATIVES

Qualify, Please Qualify 53
Winning Me Over 54
Don't Cross the Line 55
Lies Some of Us Sometimes Tell 56
The Long Reach of the Grim Reaper 57
Poses of the Imposter 58
Express Yourself 59
Complain Plus 60
What to Do 62
What to Take When 63
Musings 64

DECLARATIONS

Voices 69
Murderers 70
Chasm 71
Abstract and Concrete 72
The Flag and the Poor 73
Validation 74
Last March 75
The Science of Listening 77
Same Goal? 78
Dollars at the Dollar Store 79
A Tribute to Unknown Civil Rights Workers 80
Speaking the Wish 82
The Washerwoman 83
Emmett Till—Once More and Again 85
Not Knowing What to Say 86
On Means of Coping 87
Ignorance May Not Be Bliss 88
Hurts 89
Another Misunderstanding 90
Suspend Disbelief 92
Points 93
Welfare 94
A Gimmick 95
Not Winning 96
Your Way 97
One Step After Another 98
False Dilemma 99
A True Story 100
Health Matters 101

My Declaration 102
Fault Lines 103
Loving You PERIOD 104

INDEX 105

ABOUT THE AUTHOR 109

FOREWORD

I'll never forget the day I met Georgia—Dr. Georgia Stewart McDade, to be precise. We were in the locker room at Rainier Beach Pool in South Seattle. I was getting ready to leave quietly by and to myself. Georgia was getting ready too. By stark contrast she wasn't letting folks get away without sunshine and conversation. I overheard her chatting with everyone; some she seemed to know, others she didn't. It didn't matter. She was smiling, confident, vibrant. Her spirit filled that room. I couldn't help feel drawn to her magnetic energy. Then I overheard her say, "I was the first African-American woman to earn a Ph. D. in English from the University of Washington."

And that was it. I had to know her. Not just because she was obviously a woman warrior and pioneer (though those are certainly sufficient reasons in themselves). But also because she wasn't shy about letting a locker room full of many non-Black women know the reality of systemic racism through fusion of loving warmth, unapologetic self-assuredness, and blunt realism. As Georgia so directly puts it in "Outright Lies": "The American people are regularly fed a diet of lies. We have been betrayed more times than we can know."

I introduced myself and asked if I could interview her for a local publication called *The South Seattle Emerald*. She agreed amicably. A few days later sitting down to receive the story of Georgia's remarkable, determined life—from growing up during Jim Crow in the South to earning her doctoral degree in Seattle—became one of the most profound learning experiences and gifts of my own life. "Survived two centuries of slavery and all that entails," writes Georgia in "Just Wondering." "Endured decades of Jim Crow and all that entails...Yes."

Shortly following, we published "Georgia Stewart McDade: A Life Mightier Than Obstacles." Unsurprisingly, readership was blown away. We continued to collaborate. Georgia spoke for a Families of

Color Seattle healing group I co-organized after more Black lives lost to police violence hit the news and local families faced deepening rage and despair. Then I asked her to join me at Leschi Elementary School for an event pushing back at dominant anti-Black narratives by celebrating the triumphs and successes of Black lives. Every time, she amicably agreed. Every time, she brought her smiles, energy, and enthusiasm for life. Every time, she was a beacon for others.

Georgia is a moving intellectual, prolific writer, dedicated educator, and change agent. She is constantly out in the community attending events, encouraging others to do the same, and helping spread the word about good work. She makes a point to be where she can, whenever she can. Her energy and momentum are incomparable; her passion and artistry brim over; her enthusiasm for living and being alive are cosmic. "To be free," she writes in "Check," "do what you want to, when you want to, how you want to…"

In truth I can only dream of managing something of the same with my own time in this life and place. And so I will be forever grateful and honored to count Georgia among not only those whom I admire enormously but those I call friend. It occurs to me that we are incredibly fortunate Georgia is a writer as some of her brilliant light is captured/conveyed through her pen for all to receive. I invite you to sit in the warmth of that light now. It is my enormous privilege to share with you the many nuances and layered, gorgeous words of Dr. Georgia S. McDade.

Sharon H. Chang
Author Scholar Activist
Raising Mixed Race: Multiracial Asian Children In a Post-Racial World and *Hapa Tales and Other Lies*

INTERROGATIVES

I Am in a Hurry!

"You are always in a hurry!"
Yes. I stand accused.
"Slow down," you say.
"Relax," you say.

I understand.
I wish you understood.
If you understood, you would move, not slow me down.
But I can't, won't explain.
I'm in too much of a hurry!

You know how many sick folks I visited today?
There are many healthy folks to visit.
There are places to dine, plays to see, museums to visit.
There's reading: newspapers, magazines, newsletters, letters, e-mails,
    books to read,
And then there are responses, some required, some
    pure courtesy.
There's the writing—poems, stories, plays, articles, books.
Sometimes there is the gardening—vegetable and flower.
Add the doctors' appointments and the meetings.
Add the exercise that's supposed to be an hour but always
    takes longer.
Church gulps up a lot of time:
And then there are those chores people who live in houses
    must do and want done.
No, I do not believe I am the only busy person.
Some persons may be busier.
But I know my skills; I know what I must do. Time's running out.
Is it clear that I am in a hurry?

12/13/21

My Wants

I want to read all day—*The NY Times*, *Washington Post*, the
    few newsletters I signed up for and the many I never
    requested!
And I want to read much of what friends send me!
I want to cook that stash of new recipes from newspapers
    and friends, magazines in doctors' offices.
I want to make dishes I love to make, especially cookies.
I want to prepare workshops and lectures, give them
    regularly.
I want to quilt like M' Dear and Mama and Grandma.
I want to call friends whom I have not spoken to in ages.
I want to write my computer-less friends more often.
I want to write the good stuff and, perhaps, a bit of the bad stuff, in
    my head.
I want to swim whenever I feel like it with no thought of my hair
I want to go to the museums and art galleries, not think about cost,
    stay as long I choose.
I want to travel and travel and travel and travel some more, never
    thinking about cost, danger, or footprints!
I want most of all not to think about health and wealth and the
    same for everyone. (This is my wish list!)

Then there are chores I do not want to do but I want done:
    All the closets, especially my bedroom closet, in order
    All the cabinets, especially the pots and pans in order
    All the food pantries—and all the food in order.
    All the books—categorized, shelved, or donated.
    All the estate responsibilities—in order.

Of course, the house would always look exactly as I wish it to
    look.
Care to assist me in any way?

12/2/21

Precarity

5 begonias, $1.00 each, four die.
36 chrysanthemums, 1¢ each, 12 die.
12 lilies, in groups of three, 0 die.
Some of my many flowers survive a few days,
        others survive years.
The list and variety are interminable.
The money—no idea how much, too many losses.
The scene plays out annually.

Over the years I have watched some
        flowers survive, other flowers die.
The selection always careful, the prettiest,
        healthiest-looking flowers—they're bargains!
And yet despite the care, placement,
        nourishment, some almost always die.

I can't help thinking the same is true of people:
        despite care, placement, nourishment, some
        always die long before that 100-year mark or
        even the three score plus ten.
Look at any obituary column; visit any cemetery.
Always, always, there is no pattern.
Some have so little time in the womb, barely out
        of the womb; others make the century-plus
        mark.
The dead are dead often regardless of their action.

Oh, the questions I have!

10/30/21

Where Is He?

Like Paul, I think I've fought a good fight.
I don't hesitate to say I've almost always kept the faith.
There were a few times I wavered badly, almost collapsed: hurt,
        pain, misunderstandings, disappointments, losses.
But I always knew He was there.
Something told me He was there.
Why the internal turmoil if He's there?
I hate to admit there were times when I was sure He was
        out to lunch!
Dead? Never did that cross my mind!
I was never so distraught that I could say or think He's dead.
I was always conscious.
All I had to do was look around—places, things, people
        especially reminded me that He's alive.
He covered me over and over and over, many times
        when I was unaware or didn't take the time to say thank you.
No doubt He carried me.
Yes, God is. It's been a good haul.
I'm grateful.
I'll miss so many and so much, but I do believe there is
        so much, so many to see.
And there's beholding His face.
Yes, I'll finish the course as I leave this last cave and
        enter the perfect cave.

4/4/17

Thank You, Mr. Trump!

Never did I dream any one person could in such short
> space prove what so many have known for so long!

Prejudice, racism, discrimination, xenophobia, misogyny:
> for every person who thought any example of these was anecdotal, a misunderstanding, too sensitive, affirmative action, political correctness, or fake, you now have proof all of the above exist, may indeed thrive.

Intolerance runs rampant all over and everywhere.

Now you do accept the proof—or have you come up with yet
> another reason to refute the facts?

1/22/17

What Trump Can't Do

Yes, Donald Trump as President of the United States has power, but not as much as he thinks or wants.

Trump cannot stop any of the following:

- millions of Americans and much of the world from seeing the hatred he perpetuates nor knowing how absolute and unequivocal that hatred is
- the impact of globalism, education, science, and technology
- millions of persons from discovering their heritage
- couples of different races, including royalty, from marrying white persons and producing and parenting children of color
- directors and producers from hiring people of color
- people of color from writing, publishing, filming, addressing, and making their dreams a reality
- such productions from breaking financial records
- the number of persons of color, especially women, from helping in political campaigns, running for and winning offices
- the proliferation of articles, podcasts, books being published by African Americans, Latinx, and Native Americans
- the movies, TV shows, and ads from prominently featuring people of color in countless roles of great variety instead of only servants and buffoons
- writers from depicting the unfairness
- advertisers from sponsoring
- shows starring people of color the likes of the Williams sisters, Tiger Woods, Gabby Douglas, and Simone Biles from entering and dominating "white" sports
- more than one or two Blacks being on the TV screen simultaneously—and not a football or basketball team

- girls and women of color from entering and winning beauty contests
- people of color from being positive, encouraging front page news
- the increasing number of interracial couples and their being viewed in media
- consent decrees all over the country where some officials understand the advantage of seeing and reaping the benefits of fairness
- millions of little black and brown girls and little black and brown boys and lots of little white boys and girls and millions of adults from admiring the Obamas
- the millions of Obama supporters who met on the 2008 campaign trail, became friends, and continue the friendships
- officials all over the country from continuing their work to build communities, beloved communities
- persons previously blind to and unacquainted with privilege, poverty, and police brutality from recognizing all three
- advertisers from ending their financial support of discrimination
- all the whistleblowers, especially in government
- #MeToo nor #TimesUp despite the number of women he denigrates or from whom he attempts to deflect attention, intimidate, and bribe all the people who seek and speak the truth and for whom truth is not a chameleon that changes to fit the audience at the time.

Yes, Trump has power, but not as much as he thinks or wants.
No need to tell him, he would not understand.
His name and administration may one day be used as
> the point that marked America's fastest movement to become the country it could be, the country that millions died for, have risked everything to journey here, to become part of—a truly great country.

One day perhaps he, and a much larger portion of the world, will
>	understand and acknowledge xenophobia, racism, sexism, homophobia, anti-Semitism, Islamophobia, and misogyny are wrong, have always been wrong, will always be wrong.

One day the world will see that the better off everyone is,
>	the better off all of us are.

This is encouragement!

Did you ever think about it?

Will you?

Truth, logic, honesty, civility as well as America will
>	outlast Donald Trump.

And there is nothing his tantrums can do to stop it.

11/22/19

The Last Look

On her deathbed, mind as clear as ever, she did not want to see anyone.
The truth, at least partially, is that she wanted no one to see her.
That's what she said.
She wanted no one to see her "like that."
The emaciation? Hair loss? Translucent skin?
Despite what they wanted, family and friends acquiesced.
Vanity? Selfishness? Dignity?
There is no answer as to why she made that decision.

In her place, we may indeed make the same request.
All some of us know is that she and all those loved ones missed that one last visit that she nor we might not have known was the last visit.
On other occasions loved ones wish their final gaze had not been upon the shell of what used to be.
How can one—the living or the dying—know when to let the last look be the final look and not make the one more visit that may leave an undesirable, indelible impression?
Who can know that one last look/talk may be the incentive <u>to</u> change a life forever?

3/16/17

A Good Catch

You know how we throw babies into the air.
You know how babies jump off whatever into our arms.
The babies are always giggling.
Sometimes we have ended the game, are walking away, but the
      babies want to play.
Never ever does it occur to them that they won't be caught.
They don't know they may not be caught.
Sometimes we catchers aren't looking or had stopped the game,
      yet when they jump, we catch.
I've never seen a baby dropped.
One day a little girl, at least six years old, saw me at church,
      came running and jumped upon me as she often did when
      I was in Nikes during the week. I had on heels! I do not
      know why both of us did not fall!
I caught her.

I want a world like that.
Laugh at me.
Say what you wish or will.
At least you know what I want.
At least.
I want to jump however, whenever, from wherever.
I want to be caught.
I catch folks all the time, even when I don't want to.
Won't someone catch me?

10/4/21

They Do Not Know What They Do

"Father, forgive them; for they know not what they do."
>You know Jesus said this to the persons crucifying Him,
>but I think He also had in mind those persons who condemned Him, and some folks say He was speaking of all of us.

But the world is full of folks who hurt, kill without knowing what they are doing, at least not on the most important level:

Shoplifters
Graffiti vandals
Bullies of all ages, genders
Framing innocent persons
Denying the truth of testimonies
Kidnappers
Entertainers who encourage fans to ignore security
Girls—or women—who get pregnant to keep the boys—
>or men

Boys—or men—who damage condoms
Anybody who lies about using contraception
Grandparents who place babies up for adoption minus
>the consent of parents

Women who won't tell men they have fathered babies
Men who won't reveal they have other families
Parents who knowingly abandon children
People who play with guns
People who deny victims' stories
People who blame victims
People guilty of homicide, fratricide, matricide
People who die by suicide

The folks who came up with the idea of robbing Africa
        of its peoples and transporting them to the "New
        World," enslaving them
People who make laws designed to exclude portions of
        the populations
(This is a short list.)

Of course, perpetrators know exactly what they are doing—on
        the most immediate, superficial level.
On another level, possibly multiple levels, perpetrators know
        not what they are doing, have done!

The pain and heartache may mount without surviving
        perpetrators having any idea or thought about the action;
        other times, perpetrators are long dead as their actions
        continue to impact generations.
When the actors see another level, have another level pointed
        out to them and see the harm, often irreparable, they may
        be a bit sympathetic. When did sympathy ever banish pain?
(In little kids sometimes the pain goes away, but the hugging may be the medicine.)

There's something to the idea of treating others as we ourselves
        wish to be treated.
Now, if only all of us, ok, more of us, could take the time to
        consider possible outcomes/consequences prior to
        acting....

11/21/21

Asking for Help

Why didn't you tell me?
> I didn't want to bother you.
> I asked you the last time.
> You helped me the last time.
> I hate asking you.
> I know I didn't make a good choice.
> You told me not to.
> I was embarrassed, ashamed.

As a result of any one of the replies above, the situation
> may remain as it is or worsen.

Occasionally, but rarely, the situation may independently
> improve itself.

Why not aim to make it better? Sooner?
Being alive means possibility.
And often the situation can be rectified, improved, changed—
> especially with help.

8/8/16

Acceptable?

"Violence is not acceptable" in our society say the President,
        Congresspersons, law enforcement officers.
"You're right," say the forty-nine dead in Orlando.
"Agreed," say the nine dead in Charleston.
"Definitely," say the unarmed dead all over the USA.
"Violence is not acceptable," echo the many violently
        killed over the ages.
Mr. James Hodgkinson* accepted that statement—until
        the day he could not accept that violence is not acceptable
        and he himself began more of that not acceptable violence.
He could no longer take the mental violence.
He's white, so he'll most likely be adjudged mentally ill.
Surprisingly, he was "taken down" say some news accounts.
The violence will continue, despite the label "acceptable"
        or not, until we honestly discover, examine, and
        remedy the inequity in our society, until we
        adequately provide for the sound and the mentally ill.
Republicans and Democrats, residents everywhere must present
        and implement solutions.
Or, we select the alternative default—more violence.
I'm betting that, for a long time, the violence continues.
Care to cover my bet?

6/14/17

James Hodgkinson is the Bernie Sanders supporter and Donald Trump/Republican hater who shot five Republicans practicing for a baseball game June 15, 2017. He died at the scene.

A Chance?

What if the poor—the hungry, naked, homeless, ill, imprisoned, for example—are here to give us not-so-poor the opportunity to provide relief?

What if the disabled are decoys here to give the able bodies the opportunity to fulfill needs?

What if everybody helped anyone who lacks food, clothing, shelter, medical care, and education?

What if everyone had a job with wages to supply the above?

Don't you think crime would be reduced significantly?

Don't you?

8/24/17

Crispus Attucks

Runaway slave Crispus Attucks was the first person of five
        to die in the Boston Massacre, precursor to the
        American Revolution.
Lawyer and future President John Adams called Attucks
        and the four men killed along with him "unruly,"
        said soldiers were "forced" to fire. (Afraid for their lives?)
The soldiers were acquitted—self-defense says at least one source.
Interestingly, future Founding Father Samuel Allen claimed
        Attucks was "leaning on a stick."
Some say the segregated laws were waived so Attucks
        could be buried with others killed that day.
Then as now, questions remain about much of Attucks' life and
        death.
Not debatable was his death at the hands of British soldiers.
Not debatable was he the first in a long line of many firsts.
It would take about six years for the country to be free of British
        rule.
It would take almost a century for those like him to be free.
Unarmed men and women shot down by men in uniform is reality.
How many will die before the dream Crispus Attucks must have
        had becomes a reality?

6/14/17

Whose America?

People want their country back
I'm trying to get a country I can call mine and stop saying
      I love my country but...
What if the country you want back is the country I want
      to eliminate?
If what is great for you and terrible for me, we can have
      no compromise.

Still, I believe America can be that America so many
      dreamed of, so many—here and abroad—dream of.
There's enough proof for me to know this America is a
      reality for some.
I hear wonderful speeches of what America stands for.
But I see and I know America does not always stand for
      what America can be.
America does not stand for everyone all the time.

Am I asking too much?
If yes, why?
If no, why isn't the dream a reality, especially for those
      who followed and follow the rules?

8/24/16

What They Do

They shoot horses.
They kill wolves.
They club seals.
They trap coyotes.
They euthanize dogs and cats.
They crush beavers.
They slaughter pigs and cows.
They harpoon whales.
They poison rats—and unintentionally kill the squirrels!
Various sources say Wildlife Services legally kill millions
       of animals each year.
There must be at least 100 ways to destroy animals.
Never mind what animals endure before they die,
       nor that these particular dead animals were not the target.
Selectivity is not the number-one goal.

Why should I then be surprised when, for whatever reason and
       regardless of guilt or mental state, they kill people?
We're all animals. Right?

4/25/16

The Absence of a Presence

How do you rid yourself of a presence?
You deface it.
What it means to you may not be what it means to another.
And neither is necessarily wrong or right.
Collisions are often unintended.
When you return, you define again.
Return often enough and you may, must redefine.
Return long enough and you see the absence of your presence.
Its picture and sound exist in your mind.
Call on your memory.
Remember that nothing remains the same.
Cannot your memory, your ability to recall offer comfort?

9/9, 23/06

Inspired by works of Thomas Ager and David Traylor

What's American — Or Not

Some folks protest Colin Kaepernick's taking a knee to protest the
    murder of people of color.
Some of these folks would not, do not protest the killings.
Ronald Reagan supporters say he went to Philadelphia,
    Mississippi, because many people would be at the Neshoba
    County Fair.
Many people, especially Blacks, say Reagan chose the Mississippi
    site—seven miles from Philadelphia—because it is where
    three Civil Rights workers were killed. This choice sent a
    message to Black people: stay in your place.
Mrs. Michelle Obama plants a garden at the White House. "A great
    act" say many who have gardens or a garden for the first time.
"She does not need a garden; the first Black First Lady; she's
    acting like a servant rather than chief occupant."
Trump supporters are xenophobes, Islamophobes sexists, racists,
    misogynists say persons who don't support Trump; Trump
    supporters say they are none of these things—they don't
    agree with his comments; they themselves have been
    ignored and wish to be treated fairly, or, as Jon Stewart
    says, "Trump supporters want affordable insurance premiums."
"American" seems to be what the speaker says "American" is.
The definition changes.
In the land of the free and home of the brave, who gets to define
    the noun or the adjective "American"?

11/17/16

Want to Judge?

You say you know me.
You think you know me.
I'm sure you know only one or two parts of me, if that much.
This is no one's fault; this is as it is.
There's not enough interest!
There's not enough time if there were enough interest!!
I play many roles, most of which I enjoy.
But when you see a sliver and decide this is all I am, well there is a
    good chance you've seen just the sliver.
You may or may not have questions.
Questions don't always come in a place to ask or be given answers.
You don't always ask the questions or get answers you expect or
    want.
You don't always immediately think of the questions for which
    you wish to know answers.
Sometimes questions come as you're walking away.
Other times questions come a day or so later.
Still other times, questions come MUCH later.
And I admit, everything I've said about you can be said about me!
We can't know everything.
We often say, "I have enough information to make a judgement!"
True! True.
You can always make a judgement.
But is the judgement correct?

11/8/16

EXCLAMATIONS

Journeys

Always a journey
Moving to and fro
Knowing the destination
Unaware of a, the destination
Anticipating the arrival
Bemoaning the arrival
But moving, always moving
Leaving home
Looking for a home
Arriving home
Seeing, examining all the places in between
There's nothing like a journey
Absolutely nothing
Except, possibly, setting out on yet another journey!

8/10/16

Reclaiming Time

I wish I could get time back.
Searching for items galore: keys, shoes, books, poems,
    articles, gadgets, recipes—surely you know.
Rewinding and fast-forwarding
Replacing information I misplaced
Standing in lines
Deleting spam
Answering a telemarketer—often
Searching for what someone else moved or misplaced
Learning yet another phone or computer procedure
Trying to get the computer to place or remove a word or picture
Resending information to persons who misplaced it
Waiting for something to begin or end
Hoping the Mac beach ball spinning will stop
Going or remaining somewhere because courtesy demands it
Waiting in traffic
Looking for the right card, paper, poem, book, outfit, shoes, etc.
Writing or making comments that won't be read or heeded
Standing by for radio callers to get out their question—especially
    when it is not a question

I do not know how much time I have spent.
I know only that my time is being spent.
I know I want it back!

12/15/18

Trapped in an Era

Sometimes some of us are more stuck in an era than we may know
>because we were born into it or reared by persons who were born into or lived through it.

We're caught in an orbit around this era and can't easily escape its pull.

Consider a history of enslavement.

Think about growing up with a chronically ill parent or disabled sibling.

Depending on where they are, the Cold War babies, for instance, some do not trust Russia or the USA and are forever on guard; they want to fight; they can never get enough weaponry; weaponry can never be sufficiently sophisticated; cost is rarely a deterrent. For some Americans of a certain age, Russia will always be the enemy; some Russians of the same age feel the same.

War Zone children know only the sounds and destruction of war.

Depression-era babies, for example, are always saving. Their lives may be ever so contradictory. They do not want to spend money, but they will spend so they can be prepared "the next time."

Protesters, often consumed with protesting, think everything can be solved via protesting. Very much aware of their position, they can see what's lacking but no logic for being denied what's lacking.

Most of us take on the characteristics of the era in which we are born; we have no choice.

Though we may miss other parts of life because we concentrated on our eras, we have no choice—unless a soul from another era invites, guides, shows, pushes us into another era.

Or, we may quite consciously ignore our peers and do the opposite, thereby escaping the trap!

12/17/16

A Hog Speaks: Wall Street Humans

"Wall Street has gone hog wild," you say.
Well, I speak for hogs today.
Saying people on Wall Street went hog wild is an insult to hogs!
It's a stereotype such as Blacks are lazy or Native Americans
        are alcoholics or Jews are stingy.
No doubt there are members of these groups about whom such
        comments may be true.
But to say the description fits every member of the group is
        prejudice and not true!

Someone somewhere probably saw hogs going wild, and
        the label stuck.
A hog would never do what some of those Wall Street humans did:
        lied, stole, ruined people's lives.
Greed and power were/are the masters of these humans.
And they are arrogant.
Their lifestyles were not the least bit altered as they were crushing
        the lifestyles of so many who could never have imagined
        how some Wall Street humans live.
Not one of them lost life savings, job, house(s).
Their kids did not change colleges or drop out.
And these Wall Streeters think nothing of the millions who could
        not/cannot say the same.
And those Wall Street humans didn't go to jail.
The Obama Administration's Dodd-Frank Act is supposed to
        check the activity of these humans, but Donald Trump
        has labeled Dodd-Frank a disaster and vows to repeal it.
Indeed, some humans committed crimes, but they are above the
        law.
It takes Bernie Sanders to explain exactly what those humans did.
Remember it is they not hogs who trampled people.

Call this activity what it is: human wild, maybe human norm.

Admittedly, Jesus did cast demons from a human into pig at the demons' request.

But those pigs went directly to the lake where they drowned!

They hurt no one.

So, leave us hogs out of this Wall Street robbery.

Please, there is no connection.

Don't give hogs a bad name.

Wall Street folks went human wild.

Humans, claim your work.

Wall Street humans went human wild; they did not go hog wild!

2/1/17

Inspired by the felt painting *Hog of Wall Street* by Esther Ervin

What Can't and Can Be Imagined

Despite the absence of supposed boundaries on the imagination,
I cannot imagine what it must have been like to be stolen from
> home, bound, stuffed in the hold of a ship, moved to an alien world.

My imagination can't sail to the shores of another Continent.
But my imagination is useless when I try to imagine what being
> auctioned must have felt like.

My imagination fails again when I try to imagine what being
> installed in a new "home" was like.

I can't imagine being separated from my mom, my siblings,
> what it would have felt like when the realization became clear that I might never see them again, that I would not see them ever again.

I try, but my imagination cannot encompass the meaning of the
> Emancipation Proclamation for the enslaved..

I'm lost trying to imagine being designated 3/5 of a person;
> today I cringe.

However, I need no imagination for separate but equal.
I well remember the inequality; my imagination failed to prepare
> me for the time it would take to implement barring separate but equal.

I need no imagination for responding to Brown vs Board of
> Education; this third grader thought only of leaving her beloved school. (Don't Black kids always leave?). Never could I have imagined I would've nearly completed a Master of Arts by the time the law became reality in my neighborhood.

I needed no imagination for the passage of the Civil Right Acts of
> '64 and '65 but never could I have imagined their being gutted nearly fifty years later.—by the Supreme Court!

I lacked the imagination to think an African American
    could be elected President and never imagined
    the not so insidious blindsiding consistently
    delivered by so many in Congress and around the country.
I need no imagination when I see the wealthy, especially
    those representing "the people," those who elevate their
    interests as they trample the interests of so many with so
    much less.

What I imagine has no effect on its becoming or
    not becoming a reality.
Much of what the imagination can conceive does not become a
    reality.
What the imagination can't conceive can become a reality.
Odd how imagination works or doesn't!

12/16/1

The Color of One's Skin

How many hated being black as tar?
Who loved being high yellow/"yeller?"
Biological siblings different colors
A fact always apparent to the darker sibling
A fact often apparent to the lighter sibling
already aware of a truth.
Cousins and friends of a lighter or darker hue
Selected or excluded all because of melanin
No way could slave catchers and sellers, owners and overseers have known the power of their imprint nor the turmoil their actions would forever cause.

10/26/21

Undeserved Guilt

To a friend, the big sister revealed her failure in rearing
    her little sister.
The friend had questions:

    "Is she an alcoholic?"
    "No."
    "Is she a drug addict?"
    "No."
    "Is she pregnant?"
    "No."
    "Did she graduate?"
    "Yes."

Hoped-for responses to each question made the friend reply,
    "Many parents can't respond as you did."
Once again, a view shared relieves guilt or, at least, presents a
    different picture!

8/18/16

Futility of Worry

I worry. I worry. I worry.
Will the family be ok?
Will everyone get here?
Will we get the right leader?

Will I finish?
Will I finish on time?
Will anyone like it?

Will anyone buy it?

Again, I could go on ad infinitum!
And then I stop.
I think about what they told me when I was a little girl.
Matthew 6:25 -34.
I remember it well.
I sometimes worry so such that I realize worrying changes nothing.
Nothing!
And I realize my worrying has changed nothing!
Worry is not work!
Work requires that something move.
My worrying moves nothing.
Oh, I may pace, cry, scream
I may get a headache.
But the subject of my worry remains the same.
The subject remains the same.
Maybe that is the secret.
Leave it to God.
I've seen fat birds that never work—just flying around.
I've seen flowers that never toil or till the soil—just beaming
So, I won't worry.
I will work at not worrying--until the next time the need arises!

12/11/21

Minds and Marriage

"Let me not to the marriage of true minds admit impediments."
Shakespeare got it right.
If minds married, we would be happy more often and longer.
If minds married, we would walk and talk together easily.
If we could get minds together, we could stay together.
Getting pelvises together first rarely requires great effort.
And we often want pelvises together before we know anything
      about minds.
In the afterglow we learn minds are far apart.
We say, "I didn't know you thought that way."
We say, "Surely you don't believe that!"
We say, "I can't live like that."
We say, "I won't live like that."
And sometimes no work can get minds together.
Yes, if we married minds, we, and millions of children, would
      testify the marriage of true minds ward off, demolish
      impediments.

10/26/21

Seeing the Light

Some people have light in the morning.
Some people have light in evening.
Not surprisingly, these people see the world differently.
How nice that they sometimes come together, showing
        each other what the other sees and has seen.
How wonderfully, amazingly supreme!

8/24/16

Capital Punishment

What is capital punishment good for?
How many innocent people have been killed?
What contributions could those persons have made?
Further, killing a person or persons has yet to bring back the
        dead.
Perhaps there is a bit of satisfaction for the grieving.
But there's a good chance that the satisfaction is temporary.
Soon the mind of the aggrieved returns to the loss.

Murder is bad.
So, the State murders someone who murdered someone.
I must stop attempting to make sense of the senseless.

11/18/21

Not the One

One said he couldn't learn another culture.
Another said he couldn't go to all those plays.
One said he had nothing.
Another said he doubted if her closet were large enough for his
    clothes.
One thought his whiteness was everything.

Not one response was an answer to her question.
She had not been asked to marry, nor had she asked one to marry
    her.
But each comment assured her she was not speaking to the right
    one!

3/10/11

Resiliency

Someone is always saying someone is resilient:
        children, military families, poor people.
I know we are resilient.
I know we must be resilient if we wish to survive!
But I'll reveal a secret: I am tired of being resilient!
As I said, I know I must be resilient.
Many of us wouldn't be here if someone had not been resilient.
I know I've been resilient; I am resilient.
What I do not know is why there is so much that makes
        me resilient, requires that I be resilient so often.
I am tired of being resilient!
But knowing myself, I'll continue to be resilient.
My resiliency may be all someone else needs to overcome
        whatever whenever.
Perhaps others can be less resilient because I have been resilient.
I'll give one more for the community.
Never would I say resiliency is overrated.
But resiliency is overworked—usually by those who are not resilient.
Oh, to rid the world of the term "resilient" and the act of being
        resilient!

12/19/16

Thanks, 63,000,000

Thanks for voting for Hillary Clinton.
I do not know why you voted for her.
I do not know who or how many among you held your
        nose and voted.
I do not know who or how many voted because of her name.
I do not know who or how many voted because of her husband.
What I know is you did not vote for someone who so often lied,
        someone who not just changed his mind but said he had not
        said what he said despite video and audio to the contrary.
You refused to vote for someone who offended, insulted,
        denigrated millions of people numerous times.
You lost the election.
But in a very important way you won.
Winning, however, can have its disadvantages:
        explaining your victory to the 60,000,000 and spending the
        time to get as many as you can to accept the explanation.
You are working for the good.
You are up to the task.
You, your progeny, and millions more will survive and thrive
        because of your action despite not winning the election.

1/5/17

Randomness of the Grim Reaper

She's the caregiver, the manager; he's the long-term ill one,
        dementia.
She died at sixty-two; he's alive at seventy, memory loss forever.

Her husband died in 1942; she lives, no friends, no relatives.

A mother of four is killed by a drunk driver.

He's smoked more than sixty years; she never touched a cigarette.
She died at fifty-three; he, aged seventy, lives, never thinking he
        may quit smoking.

At seventy, she never exercises; at fifty, he continues a routine
        began at sixteen.
She lives; he died—at fifty-one.

He's slender; she's much more than plump.
He dies at forty-six; she's in her sixties.

Forget reason, logic, fairness; they have no place here.
Once again we humans are forced to admit that so often
        we have little or no control on this unlevel field.

8/17/16

Morning Greetings

An older woman and a young man headed to opposite
>sides of the street.
"Good Morning!" said the woman.
"What's good about it?" said the young man.
The woman stopped in the middle of the street: "You can say,
>'What's good about it? You can see across the street. You know when to cross the street. Shall I continue?"
"No, mam," said the young man. "Good Morning!"

5/15/18

An Outsider Speaks

How many ways can we be outsiders?
Legion.
        The only woman, man in this group
        The only African American, Asian, etc. in the group.
        The only degreed individual in the room.
        The only Southerner, Northerner, Midwesterner, etc.
        The only Las Vegas visitor going to a casino, church,
        The only one not wearing a store-bought dress.
        I could continue ad infinitum.

I know now that outsiders aren't always noticeable.
I know sometimes outsiders are more aware than insiders.
Outsiders, however, may create problems, bigger problems for
        the insiders.

I know now that being the outsider can be good or bad.

I often manage without knowing I'm an outsider.
Other times I manage because I'm the outsider.
In either case I may or may not do exceedingly well.
Perhaps having this information increases awareness.
Perhaps having this information encourages.
Perhaps having this information emboldens.
Perhaps armed with such information at least one outsider will step
        up more often, less fearful, more certain.
Or perhaps the outsider would relish nothing more than
        shuffling off the outsider traits.

6/12/11

Preoccupied with Horror

"Annie is no more. There is no Annie."
Those are the words of a young sibling whose five-year-old sister
     is missing and presumed dead.

Perhaps an adult told the child, "Annie is no more. There is no
     Annie."

What could Annie have done to be no more?
Nothing!
Nothing.
Like the Sandy Hook children
Like the Oxford children
Like the Pilchuck children
Like the Columbine children
I will not lengthen this list with more specifics.

Like all the adults who perished with the children

Like all the murdered spiritually, mentally, physically

You know what's on my mind.

So many of us mourn, will forever mourn.

> PERSON should be more.
> PERSON should be here.
> PERSON should be.

And I am always sad because I want all of them to be more, be
     here.
They should be here.
And yet, they are no more.

12/14/21

Being

Admittedly, it may be argued,
> I am patient,
> I am tolerant,
> I am understanding,
> I am flexible,
> I am agreeable.

And yet, more and more I need to be more of each of the above
> plus at least one unknown.

What I have is often insufficient, inadequate to combat
> the seriousness and the wiles of others.

Always it seems I must be on guard.
Folks with whom I have no argument want to argue.
Never pretending to be easy, I am far from the difficulty of
> what I think is a Sunday morning hangover.

There are times when I call on the words of Curtis Mayfield:
> "Let me be! Let me be! Let me be!"

6/11/16

Pie Chart of My Life

I look at my life like a sliced pie, a whole pie but a pie cut in
    unequal wedges.
Family gets a chunk, more than one slice.
Friends get another chunk.
Foes take a piece, not much.
Exercise is more than a sliver.
Theater is a healthy hunk.
Reading maintains a great portion.
Studying gets a share.
Housework always takes too big of a piece.
Shopping has a little part.
Writing has a more than ample slab.
Travel is a huge section.
Church has a bigger than average part.
Miscellaneous has a minute yet ever-present, sometimes varying
    segment.

I know the pie must stay whole, but I'm determined to
    cut some of those slices differently!

2/13/19

The Day the Pill Went on the Market

The feeling of warmth from the first fire
The taste of meat from the first barbecue
The realization of Helen Keller when she tastes and
    names water
The thrill of Neil Armstrong when he set foot on the moon
This is not for all women but for many women: the significance of
    the birth of the pill.

Imagine what must have gone through the minds of women when
    they learned taking a pill could prevent pregnancy!
Imagine being able to plan to have a baby—or not.
Imagine deciding the number and spacing of babies.
Imagine realizing that neither making love nor having
    sex meant making a baby.
Imagine how much time preoccupied a man and a woman
    wondering if and waiting for a sign no baby
    was in the making.
Imagine being able to begin or advance a career
    without considering becoming pregnant.
Imagine how much better sex must have become when
    fear of pregnancy disappeared.
The pill left its mark in ways still being reckoned:
    fewer deaths from childbirth; improved longevity; planned
    family size; women's financial contributions to the family,
    community, society.
But the biggest news, the greatest news is the number of women
    who gained control over their bodies.
More than ever before, women could choose when to become
    pregnant!
At least much of the world's population sighed gratefully.

2/6/18

An Addendum

More women got the gravity of the pill's introduction
        before men did. (I want to say DUH!)
But then, women bore the larger burden, always had
        more to lose than men.
Yet many women and men failed to realize the pill's
        liberation for men!
Significantly reduced are marriages to "do the right thing."
Fewer men ask, "Is it mine?"
Fewer men reply, "It is not mine!"
Fewer men respond, "I'll pay for the abortion."
Disappearing acts all but cease—at least because of pregnancy.
Maybe time cannot possibly tell exactly what the pill did
        to and for civilization.
But no one argues that the pill did not permanently affect society.

1/29/18

The pill has had a dramatic impact on social life in the US, affecting women's health, fertility trends, laws and policies, religion, interpersonal relations, family roles, women's careers, gender relations, and premarital sexual practices. Some would say the emergence of the women's rights movement of the 1960s and 1970s was significantly related to the availability of the pill and the control over fertility it enabled.

That Look

Some folks never give anyone that look.
Some folks never have anyone give them that look.
Some folks give that look.
Some folks get that look.

For the few who need to know, here are a few couples
    who give and get that look TO EACH OTHER, AT THE SAME TIME:
Furillo and Davenport ("Hill Street Blues")
Steve and Alice ("Another World")
Brian and Audrey ("Things We Lost in the Fire")
But they are in films; good actors do it easily.

Real people Barack and Michelle Obama give and get it.
Remember the most viewed selfie
    THAT NO ONE REQUESTED WE TAKE OR DOWNLOAD?
Folks just wanted it.
Neither Barack nor Michelle asked that it be posted.
Neither Barack nor Michelle asked that the picture be taken.
Neither knew that the picture was being taken.

Anyone who has been in love and loved at the same time
    knows that look.
Each time that look is seen or mentioned, folks get it.
They recognize it. They understand it. Many envy it.
Extremely blessed are those who simultaneously give
    and get that look.

2015

Degrees of Strange

'Tis strange, passing strange how few people consider how
many people are on earth at any one moment.
But stranger is how little we know about the few people
we regularly see daily in one week.
Strangest, however, is how rarely we know people we
see daily and nightly in our household.
'Tis strange, ever so strange.

12/5/20

IMPERATIVES

Qualify, Please Qualify

Say what we mean whenever.
We can create problems for others and ourselves when we say
 what we mean.
We can create as many or more problems for others
 and ourselves if we do not say what we mean.
There's no guarantee a listener hears and understands what we say.
But we can reduce the degree and number of misunderstandings if
 we qualify.
"Mexicans," for instance, means "all Mexicans."
Some Mexicans, many Mexicans, fewer Mexicans, Mexicans from
 Jalisco, and Mexicans I know are all smaller groups than
 "Mexicans."
Substitute "Muslims," "Blacks," "Jews," "children," or "women"
 for "Mexicans."
In each instance a different number of persons is involved.
Numbers matter.
Qualify please.
Please qualify.
We can solve some problems if we qualify.

12/29/16

Winning Me Over

Homemade French vanilla ice cream

Sweet potato pie

Coconut cake

My peanut brittle

New York cheesecake

Scoop du Jour strawberry malt

Yellow cake with chocolate icing

Boehm's turtles

Homemade apple pie

Baby Ruth candy bars

Your chance of winning me over is significantly increased by the number of items you give me from the above list.

5/7/16

Don't Cross the Line

Don't cross that line.
Dare you.
Double-dog dare you!

Beware drawing a line in the sand—or anywhere else.
The brilliant, bold, bumptious Julius Caesar knew what he was
        doing when he crossed the Rubicon.
He knew where he was; he knew who he was.
He did not say what he was going to do, no need to.
He acted.

Too many folks talk but won't, don't, can't act.
Usually better to set boundaries within and live up to them than
        blurt dares and then back down.

2/7/18

Lies Some of Us Sometimes Tell

He ain't heavy.
I don't see color.
It doesn't matter.
I forgive.
I don't mind.
Forget it.
I've forgotten it.
Don't think about it.
I'm good. You're good. We're good.
We're straight.
You don't owe me.
I got this.
I see.
It's clear now.
I understand.
I have a previous engagement.
I'm sorry.
I'll try.
No hard feelings.
Thank you.
No problem.
Ok.

These replies are civil.
These replies may be the right thing to do or what we've been
    taught and told to do.
But these replies often create more problems than they solve
    because these replies may be lies.

8/8/16

The Long Reach of the Grim Reaper

My maternal grandmother Mama
My first Pastor Rev. Bowie
My pastor Rev. Himes
My mother M'Dear
My principal Mr. M. H. Carroll
My big brother Jr.
My teacher Mr. Grant
My friend Sandra
My friend Woody
My friend Charles

No one knows the impact of the deaths of each of the above.
No one knows what can rock a world nor how much.
Each time I think I have the impact figured out, am over the pain,
       something takes me back, stands me still.
If only I could know there's a time, the end of the memories,
       I think I could manage better.
But shortly and unexpectedly I have other names to add to this
       limited list, and the Reaper continues the work, ignorant of
       my cares and pain.

5/7/16

Poses of the Imposter

The imposter poses all the time.
Whatever one needs, the imposter can be.
Sometimes the imposter convinces us to get what we don't need!
Protean
Chameleon
We do not have a chance—unless, of course, we too
        are quick-change artists as adept as the imposter.

It's been my experience that everyday inexperienced,
        unsuspecting, honest persons lack such skills.
Therefore, their rate of success is significantly different
        from the success of the imposter.
Beware the imposter though the imposter's skills usually
        outwit those of the ever so large pool of the unsuspecting.
Know that such a monster never looking monstrous exists.

2/7/18

Express Yourself

Express yourself!
Express yourself.
You're entitled to your opinion.
Express yourself.
People died for freedom of expression.
Just know that your expression is neither warranted nor wanted
    by every listener.
The opinion may be right, wrong, beneficial,
    baseless, illogical, etc.
Sometimes this does not matter.
However, know that you may be called upon to defend your
    expression, go to war for it.

12/19/19

Complain Plus

"I can't complain. What can I do?"
"Much" was my response.
You can indeed complain.
In no order, select a suggested activity:
You can rail.
You can shop.
You can meditate.
You can take a walk.
You can go to a park.
You can light a candle.
You can get a massage.
You can go on vacation.
You can listen to music.
You can clean something.
You can call or visit a friend.
You can take the train or bus.
You can pray, sing, or dance.
You can read a poem or a book.
You can swim or go to the gym.
You can write a letter or a poem.
You can travel an unfamiliar route.
You can visit a rehabilitation center.
You can go to a seed and garden store.
You can treat yourself to a lavish meal.
You can go get a manicure and/or pedicure.
You can visit an orphanage or nursing home.
You can contribute to or work at a food bank.
You can clean a closet with Goodwill or Value Village in mind.

Look at the people who hurt people rather than complain.
They hurt persons they know; they hurt persons they do not know.
Some hurt themselves too.

Please know there's much that can be done instead of or in
        addition to complaining!
Go for the good choices.
Please go for the good choices.
The world needs millions more to go for the good choices.

12/17/16

What to Do

I didn't do anything when your mom died
I didn't do anything when you attempted suicide.

I regret that I didn't do anything.
I probably always will regret not doing anything.
I couldn't do anything I now realize.
I didn't know what to do.

Perhaps one day you'll know how one may function, function,
        function without doing what needs to be done,
        that sometimes folks can be so busy because they don't
        don't know what to do.
The love is there, never left.
The love remains.
But love does not mean always knowing what to do.

10/28/21

What to Take When

Someone can humiliate you once.
You can't prepare for that—you couldn't have known.

You can ride with the drunk person once.
Yes, the drinker was wrong—and you had no idea.

The abuser can hit you once.
Yes, still wrong—whatever the "reason."

You must protect yourself always—in and under all circumstances.
You know about self-preservation.
You must now learn the true meaning of love.
The verb love far exceeds the value of the noun love.
There are no rehearsals, practice games in real life.
Some of us don't receive the modeling, teaching, preaching,
        nurturing, reading we need as early as we need it.
And we can't always be helped if we don't sound alarms!
Sometimes we can't save ourselves nor others as early as we or
        they need saving.
The next time, however, if there is a next time, the odds of
        receiving and giving help should have increased
        dramatically.

10/26/21

Musings

People often say, "Thank you for waiting."
I want to respond, "I did not willingly wait; you held me hostage."

4/6/12

We can't have it all. Surely everyone has heard it, been reminded of it. Some have learned to live comfortably with the realization. Others have not and spend much irreplaceable time trying to get whatever it is they call all.

8/24/16

Why should Congresspersons and some American citizens be so surprised that a Filipino leader disrespects the president of the United States when so many of them have disrespected the president of the United States since the day he was elected, have disrespected him almost eight years and show no sign of halting?

9/9/16

I'm always fascinated that parents, teachers, ministers, coaches and Scoutmasters, among others, save so many children but not their own.

10/2/16

Jim Wallis is one of the most rational persons I have read lately. Here is one of his quotes: "Last year, Americans spent $450 billion on Christmas. Clean water for the whole world, including every poor person on the planet would cost about $20 billion. Let's just call that what it is: A material blasphemy of the Christmas season."

11/16/16

Brilliant Jon Stewart says all the people who voted for Donald Trump are not a monolith, i.e. all of them are not racists, xenophobes, Islamophobes, sexists, etc. Says he, "They just want lower insurance premiums!" Does he not think those who voted for Clinton not want lower insurance premiums? Surely Stewart knows Clinton supporters want jobs that pay a livable wage. I think most of the people in this country want basically the same: food, clothing, shelter, medical care, education—the American Dream. This is especially true for the millions who are missing all or some of the named wants. What I wonder is why so many millions—politicians on all sides included—so willingly and willfully sacrifice others to get what they want while preventing others from getting much less or none of the same. Millions never saw the Dream inscribed "Whites Only." More, the Dream has been advertised around the world.

Have you ever heard of a Bangladesh Dream? Norwegian Dream? Brazilian Dream?

11/18/16

Decades ago I met a man at a party one night. He told me BASICALLY men don't change; they get a woman who stays for as long as she can. After she leaves, the men get a younger woman. After she leaves, the men get someone younger still. He said men marry thinking women won't change, and women marry thinking men will change. I add "basically" to his sentence! He said he knew his wife—at the party—was leaving him soon. He never said anything about changing anything or trying to convince her to stay. He was waiting. When she left, he would get someone else.

8/7/21

DECLARATIONS

Voices

Do this.
Do that.
Don't you dare do this!
You must do this.
You can't do that!

What if I listened to my voice only?
Granted, there might be mistakes, big mistakes.
But enduring the consequences of my choices is easier
> than enduring the consequences of choices made by others.

All consequences are not equal.

Now, I never said I would not listen to the voices.
I will listen.
But I reserve the right to discard the voices, listen to my voice,
> make my choices.

11/2/21

Murderers

Leave your child in a car to asphyxiate because you
        want to be free.
Set your child on fire to hurt the mother.
Cook your child in an oven because you need to exorcise
        him of demons.
Drown your children to keep your "boyfriend."
Shoot your wife or husband because you don't want to be
        married anymore or you do not wish to share the wealth.
Push your husband off a cliff on the honeymoon
        because you don't want to be married.
Smother your grandparents because you want "your"
        inheritance now.
End a stranger's life because you want his car, cellphone, or
        sneakers.
Cut a child from a woman's womb because you want a baby.
Kill your classmates because …

No one can count the "reasons" humans have concocted to
        kill other humans.
After murderers reveal or we discover their acts, we don't
        know what to say, don't understand.
All of us can be grateful that these acts come from an
        extremely small minority.
 And yet the majority of us continue to do whatever we can to
        deter as much evil and prevent as much pain as we can.

11/16/17

Chasm

There's a chasm between what I want and what I need,
    what I want to be and what I am
    what I want to do and what I do.
I hate this divide!

The chasms may have always been present.
Were they not as wide, not noticeable?
Maybe my sight was blurred.
Maybe I didn't want to make the leap.
Maybe I felt pushed.
Maybe I felt used.
And I'm not always proud of my thoughts or choices.
The simple truth: Despite all my moving, sometimes I want to
    stay where I am.

11/17/16

Abstract and Concrete

Unfortunately, many of us do not distinguish the abstract from the concrete.

We are not prejudiced.

We say we love everybody.

We say we would not hurt a fly.

This is the abstract.

The concrete requires more than simply saying I love everybody.

The concrete always requires stepping out and standing up.

So comfortable in our microcosms, we are often unaware of our biases and unwilling to report ourselves to ourselves.

Surely, we will not report others!

When our biases make the lives of others worse or kill them mentally, spiritually, and sometimes physically, we are without a doubt liars.

This concrete is opposite of that abstract we earlier professed.

Our implicit or unconscious biases make us say I disagree with another's bias, but I will do nothing.

It seems so simple to me: we work to eliminate prejudice and inequality, or all of us die on our separate sides. having lived leaner lives.

11/4/16

The Flag and the Poor

Poor Old Glory, so sad.
Everybody knows this flag.
It's been everywhere!

All over the place.
Mars!
To the moon!
Graves
Parades
Houses
Businesses
Sports events
Olympics
Boats
Ships
Planes
Cars,
Bikes and Trikes
Marches
Lapels

For the good
For the bad—a few marred and burned

And yet, the flag continues to wave, impervious to
        all we humans say it means, say it's worth.

Flag flies all over, everywhere.
Too many people never get to fly.
The flag really will be ok.
Poor people may never be ok.

We need to help poor people; there is no poor flag.

6/13/21

Validation

Validation. Validation. Validation.
So often validation is invaluable.
Some of us will do, can do all kinds of feats when we are
  validated.
But not anyone can validate us.
Validators must be trusted, respected.
And when validation comes, our superpowers often bound to
  the fore.

In my salad days, validation was a tool to make people of all
  ages accomplish good.
Now validation regularly encourages one to do wrong as
  much as it can to do evil.
Too many of us can be moved to commit terrible, dangerous,
  sometimes deadly feats when we are validated.

The validated is not always aware that a choice may build or
  destroy.

11/9/21

Last March

I will march no more forever.
The thousands of marches, the millions of people, the number of
>years…
I will not march again.
I marched in Louisiana, in Washington.
The physical distance between the states is far, 2627 miles.
But believe me when I say the mental distance is much farther.
No, I will not march again.
No longer the wide-eyed student trying to get the Fifth
>Circuit's attention on my first trip to New Orleans
No longer the hopeful adult, commemorating 25 years after the
>'63 March on Washington, nuns on one side of me,
>gays on the other in Seattle,
Interracial couples all over the place!
I couldn't help thinking how diverse, truly diverse the marchers
>are, how good this is!
So many folks seemed so happy; folks frolicked!
Civil rights, everybody has civil rights!
Everybody is now marching.
Why shouldn't everyone be involved?
But somewhere, on Third Avenue, I realized how little had
>changed: the march was much larger; there were far more
>whites; there were folks who probably detest being "other."
But juveniles and adults are still being incarcerated unjustly.
More African Americans are in jail now than South Africa jailed at
>the height of apartheid!
Some teachers say they can predict which third graders
>will go to prison.
Employment—unemployment and underemployment—housing…

Education so often so bad despite the honesty and hard work of
> many…

Voter suppression—purging, gerrymandering, fewer voting
> because of change or closing of sites, shorter voting hours, not enough machines, changing ID requirements.

Who could have guessed we would still be renewing the '65
> Voting Rights Bill in 2015, that today more states would have more ways to thwart voters, AND THAT SOME LAW MAKERS OPPOSE EXTENDING THE BILL?

Weren't voting and housing and public accommodations
> supposed to be solved in the '60s?

Much work must be done.

Definitely.

There is no space for coasting, no space for resting or being
> comfortable.

Everybody who values humanity—humanity, I say—needs to
> challenge a system that writes off folks
> because of the color of their skin, their sex, their sexual
> preference, their physicality.

I came home, put my sign in the closet—it is still there!

I will vote.

I will sign petitions, get others to sign petitions.

I will write letters.

I will inform.

I will make addresses.

I will donate money.

I will encourage and applaud others who march.

But I will not march.

I will march no more forever.

5/9/15

Inspired by a painting by Jasmine Brown and my sign in the guest room closet.

The Science of Listening

Listen.
All of us want somebody to listen.
We may not be saying anything of importance.
We may or may not know we're saying something of
    no importance.
The listener may or may not know we're saying
    something of importance.
But the speaker wants a listener.
Maybe if more of us had listeners all of us would have
    fewer problems.

10/21/16

Same Goal?

Sometimes two people want the same something.
But their methods of attaining the goal are astronomically
    different.
Neither sees nor follows the other's way.
There can be a solution.
Speak honestly to the person—and always define terms at the
    slightest hint of not being clear.
Be willing to accept another truth: you thought you
    wanted the same thing.
Knowing, realizing this truth is probably better
    now than later.

10/16/16

Dollars at the Dollar Store

The Dollar Store where everything's a dollar
And you can see people putting items aside
Items they wanted, were going to get,
Items children and grandchildren wanted.

But the adults realized they had no more dollars
Or needed those dollars for something else
Not that they hadn't worked hard,
Just that for so many of us the dollars are limited
Even when everything's a dollar.

Yesterday was not the first time I slipped the number
       of dollars needed into the hand of the shopper.
Only just now was I ashamed that I had not given her more
       dollars than she obviously needed.
I'll remember next time.

10/26/21

A Tribute to Unknown Civil Rights Workers

Thanks.
Many thanks to the many unnamed civil rights workers.
Thanks to all the people who took risks all the centuries.
Thanks to all those workers who eavesdropped on their white
    employers, employers who spoke around their servants as if
    the servants were deaf, stupid.
Thanks to all the people who gave money despite how little money
    they had.
Thanks to all the people who kept the food coming—
    purchasing, preparing, delivering, serving.
Thanks to all the people who kept the living quarters clean.
Thanks to all the people who ran errands.
Thanks to all the people, usually women, who typed, Xeroxed.

Thanks for risking losing jobs; thanks for losing jobs.
Thanks for losing family and friends—not through death—
    but because they disagreed with the cause, thought they
    themselves had a better way, or were not willing to take risks.
Thanks to all those whose loved ones were injured, sometimes
    permanently.
Thanks to all the people who were injured, sometimes
    permanently.
Thanks to all the survivors who continued the battle though their
    loved ones died.
Thanks to all of those whose lives were taken.
Thanks, great thanks go to those who had the vision to know life
    could be better for us, those who realized that they
    themselves might not reap the benefits of what they sowed
    but selflessly gave anyway.
You are in my thoughts often.
I hope you know how grateful many of us are.

I hope the day comes when the nation and world realize the high
> price you paid and the countless lives you saved.

I hope the nation will know that it is as good as it is because of
> what you and your supporters did.

And know that many of us continue the fight.

11/12/16

Speaking the Wish

What do you want me to say?
I can say that!
> (I wish I'd known, had understood. I could have said it a long time ago.)

I can say that later, perhaps.
I can't say that.
I'll tell you why.
"Honest" being my operative word, I learn so much when you
> honestly tell me what you want me to say.

7/12/16

The Washerwoman

Up very early, my grandmother Mama always rose before I did.
Never in the short times our lives overlapped did I see her
>sleeping.
By the time I was up, she had a big black pot full of boiling water
>over a roaring fire.
Some days earlier she had used that same big black pot
>to make lye soap.
All she had to do was wait until her clients brought their dirty
>clothes.
Like clockwork, the Hennekers showed up each Sunday night
>with two bundles of clothes.
Mama got the clothes out of the trunk, took them straight to the
>backyard where she sorted them and then
>slowly dropped them in the big black pot.
A while later she took a long stick and poked the clothes
>mercilessly.
How she knew when they were clean, I never knew.
Eventually she removed them from the pot, put them in a tub for
>rinsing.
She moved them to another tub filled with bluing.
She wrung the clothes, hung them on the clothesline.

By late Monday afternoon, she had taken the clothes from the line,
>folded some pieces and ironed other pieces.
Again, I was warned not to get too close to the stove nor the hot
>heavy irons heated on the stove.
By the time the Hennekers returned, their clothes were ready.
They paid her $2.00 and were on their way until Sunday
>night next week.

Mama had no complaints about the discomfort.
Mama had no complaints about the dirty, smelly work.
Mama had no complaints about the strenuous work.
This was her lot?
This was her lot.
I wish I had known to ask about the discomfort, the work, the strain.
I wish I had known to ask of what she dreamed, learned what she had endured.
Years later I realized Mama was but one more of the many who willingly, silently sacrificed so that her children and grandchildren could have a better life.
She was one more example of the great love rarely—if ever—mentioned but was always so obvious.
She was one more reason for each of us to give our best.
There's no doubt she got a well done.
She is one of the many folks who I hope would say well done about our work—perhaps not dirty but still uncomfortable and straining.

1/17/17

Emmett Till — Once More and Again

If truth be told, I should have long ago written everything I had to
    say about Emmett Till.
You do know he was brutally murdered in August of 1955?
He shows up in more of my writings than any other figure.
I think I'm through with him, and lo and behold, he's back!
I have several theories about his presence but don't know why he's
    been with me so many decades.
After seeing his coffin in the Smithsonian National African-
    American Museum of History and Culture, I thought, "OK.
    Emmett and I can rest."
But there he was in the newspaper the 28th of January 2017!
Carolyn Donham, the woman who accused the fourteen-
    year-old Emmett of threatening her, whistling at her,
    admitted to historian Timothy Tyson in 2008, "Nothing
    that boy did could ever justify what happened to him."

Donham did not want to work in the store owned by her husband.
She thought if she convinced her husband that she was afraid to be
    in the store, he himself would work in the store.
Was she wrong!

Emmett's mother always said he could never have made the
    statements he was accused of saying because he stuttered.
Some accounts say Emmett's mom herself had told him to whistle
    when he began stuttering....
We may never know the whole truth, but we do know one
    undebatable truth: Emmett Till, like thousands before him
    and hundreds after him, was murdered in cold blood.
He nor anyone else deserved to die as he did, Mrs. Donham.
Oh, I hope Emmett and his mother are resting in peace, both
    looking as beautiful as they ever did.
I hope they are looking out for all of us still down here on the
    ground, if truth be told.

2/2/17

Not Knowing What to Say

I need to say something. I have to say something. I want to say
        something.
But I don't know what to say.
I knew I would have to say something.
What do I say?
I DO NOT KNOW WHAT TO SAY!
I know I cannot not say something.
I can say something. I need to say something.
I have to say something. I want to say something.
I don't want to say the wrong something.
But what is the RIGHT something?
I know why there's a problem: I do not want you
        to have this pain, yet I know all the wanting
        in the world will neither ease nor erase the pain.
Perhaps you can tell me what to say,
        what you wish to hear.
Perhaps I can say it.
But then, that does not work.
I'm the one who must say something, to you.
Selfish me!
I want you to say something, not just anything,
        but something.
I vacillate between having nothing to say and much to say.
And the real problem is this: what I want to say is, "Please say
        something to me."
I always want you to say something.

7/9, 12/19

On Means of Coping

I've seen incidents hundreds of times, been mesmerized that two–
 ten, 100+–persons can see the same event and yet cope
 startlingly differently.
One raves; the other rants.
One responds positively, the other responds negatively.
One thinks less force was necessary; the other thinks more.
One lives better; another dies spiritually or mentally or physically.
One is energized; another is resigned.
If only we could know the key to coping healthily….

9/9/16

Ignorance May Not Be Bliss

"Nobody was supposed to get killed; I did not intend to kill nobody," said the young man on death row; he had joined friends in robbing a convenience store.

In his attempt to escape, he hit and killed a policeman.

There are the diverse ages of women who unilaterally decide to have a baby only to learn later that the man should have contributed more than sperm, his consent included.

Some men play such games too. There are the women and men who are convinced that a baby can save a relationship only to discover there is no saving of the relationship but only obligations that may worsen the couple's situation and doom a baby.

There are the persons with guns who say they have the guns to protect themselves but maim and kill loved ones accidentally, others in a fit of rage, or themselves.

There's just not enough time to make enough people devote more time to thinking before they act. What they didn't know, don't know is not always detrimental. But sometimes what they don't know is detrimental, and the consequences of such ignorance may endure forever as it variously hurts untold numbers.

9/13/16

Hurts

Sometimes people hurt us terribly, and that was their plan.
Other times people hurt us terribly, and they never had a plan,
        would swear they never intended to hurt anyone.
Either way, we have scars, different sizes, different degrees,
        but scars, nevertheless.
We can't get through life minus scars.
We can be grateful when there is someone to help the healing.
Knowing this, we can intentionally work on scarring less
        of ourselves and others by critically thinking before we
        act.
Knowing this, we can provide balms rather than pain when and
        where we can.

10/22/16

Another Misunderstanding

Michelle Obama said, "I wake up every morning in a house
    built by slaves."
Virginia Kruta said, "Anyone who is willing to work hard and
    apply one's talent in America" can be successful.
It's clear Virginia Kruta believes her truth trumps Michelle
    Obama's.
So much is embedded in the Kruta statement:
    If everyone had parents such as the Obama children and the
    Robinson* children or a mom such as Obama's or his
    grandparents ….
Anyone who works hard….
Anyone who has the talent….
Of course, everyone does not have parents like the Obamas.
Nor does everyone have the talent.
Should that preclude living a life that's basically satisfactory?
Millions of people in this country—Native, Latino, Black,
    Asian, White— work very hard, every day, seven days a
    week and never "succeed."
They do not have decent places to live, adequate medical care,
    good schools for their children, and other items Ms Kruta
    most likely had and never imagined not having.
Bill O'Reilly said the slaves who built the White House
    were "well-fed and had decent lodgings."
Where is the proof?
The implication is that slavery was not bad.
Why there is such division is clear: we are making and
    supporting different points.
Some of us are convinced slavery was and always will be wrong.
Others of us refuse to see the impact—everlasting so far.
One of my wishes is to have the latter group understand
    their gross misunderstanding.

10/23/16

*Robinson is Michelle Obama's maiden name; Craig is her brother.
Michelle Obama 6/3/16 commencement address at City College of New York

Virginia Kruta 7/27/16 Top Right News

Bill O'Reilly 7/26/16 *Politico*

Barack Obama's grandparents: Madelyn Payne (1922 - 2008) and Stanley Armour Dunham (1918 - 1992) and his mother Ann Dunham (1942-1995) reared him.

Michelle Obama's parents are Fraser Robinson III (1935 - 1991) and Marian Shields Robinson (1937 -)

Suspend Disbelief

Suspend disbelief.
The television viewer complained that Dr. House follows a
      Formula: a patient has an illness; no one can cure it; House
      comes and unorthodoxly arrives at a solution.
"The Fugitive"? "Batman"? "Superman"? "Columbo"?
If you know anything about the comics or films, you know
      the protagonist wins or puts up a valiant fight before he
      dies!
Before you begin to watch or read, you know the protagonist wins.
Suspending disbelief is part of the reading and the viewing.
Playgoers know suspending belief is part of the ticket.
No suspending, no enjoyable play-going.
You pretend there's a three-sided room where you look through the
      fourth wall; you go from Egypt to Rome in the opening of a
      curtain or look to left or right.
The practice of suspending disbelief occasionally works in real
      life.

10/7/16

Points

Walter wants to talk about his dreams;
Walter's wife Ruth wants him to eat his eggs.*
Women are from Venus; men are from Mars.**
The slave owner cannot possibly have the viewpoint of
      the slave, nor the slave that of the slave master.
Each statement is true; each statement is valuable.
The points, however, are irrelevant to the argument.
The subjects are on different playing fields, in different
      libraries, and, therefore, have different perspectives.
It's too bad.
Such differences may destroy us all.

*   Walter and Ruth Younger, from Lorraine Hansberry's play *A Raisin in the Sun* (1958)

**   *Men Are from Mars, Women Are from Venus*, by John Gray, 1994

10/7/16

Welfare

There are folks who have nothing good to say about welfare.
These folks usually have no idea that most of the people
    on welfare are children.
They do not know that most of the persons on welfare
    are white.
Some of the welfare haters say/believe it is the
    responsibility of the parent to take care of the child,
    that people should not have children
    they can't afford.
What the haters cannot know is the circumstances of the
    people who need help.
Occasionally, the haters know the stories of one or two persons and
    conclude these are the stories of the majority, if not all.
What no one knows is how many persons "qualify" for welfare but
    would never apply.
No way have they heard the women and men who say,
    "Take your welfare!" or "I don't want welfare" or
    "I'll never take welfare."
What most recipients need are good skills, educations,
    adequate health care, and living-wage jobs.
Imagine what kind of country the USA could be!
Persons responsible to "promote the general welfare"
    rarely know anything about how the 47%* plus live.
Ditto the bottom 15%.
Elected officials often have no idea remedying these problems is a
    portion of their charge.
And for those who argue "promote the general welfare" is
    not related to the humanitarian needs espoused,
    my answer is note how well we prosper as we continue
    to ignore these needs.

11/3/16

* In 2012 Presidential candidate Mitt Romney, not knowing he was being recorded, said 47% of voters do not pay income tax.

A Gimmick

I want a gimmick.
No, I need a gimmick.
Based on my age, I must change my tactics if my
    wishes are to materialize prior to my demise.
Since about age ten, I have wanted discrimination to end.
I thought it would be gone by the time I became an adult.
I was sure it would be gone.
I understand now in a way a child could never understand.
Over the years I saw discrimination morph from separate
    but equal to more subtle acts all the while interspersed with
    the killing of unarmed men and women of color.
Despite hate-free and drug-free zones, I realize legislation minus
    hearts and minds can't make my dreams materialize.
That beautiful language in the Declaration of Independence, those
    Bill of Rights—all were written without me in mind.
And despite Amendments, I still don't count.
No matter how often I remind myself, I see the reality.
As if speaking to me, The Kerner Report of 1968
    described the circumstances perfectly: "What white
    Americans have never fully understood—but
    what the Negro can never forget—is that white society
    is deeply implicated in the ghetto. White institutions
    created it, white institutions maintain it, and white society
    condones it."
In 1992, Andrew Hacker said basically the same: "So, in allocating
    responsibility, the response should be clear. It is white
    America that has made being black so disconsolate an
    estate. Legal slavery may be in the past, but segregation and
    subordination have been allowed to persist."
As much as I hate to leave this burden for others to bear and solve,
    I may be forced do just that—unless I get a gimmick very
    soon.

10/26/18

Not Winning

Mallory didn't win—he got to the top, but as one
      mountain climber said, "If you don't get back, then
      you aren't successful."
John Kennedy didn't really win—he had only a thousand days.
Challenger crew Christa McAuliffe, Gregory Jarvis,
      Judith A. Resnik, Francis R. (Dick) Scobee,
      Ronald E. McNair, Mike J. Smith, and Ellison S. Onizuka,
      lost.
We cannot always immediately tell if we have won, even
      when everything in the present says we have.

8/24/18

Your Way

Rare is the process that can be done only one way.
Yet too many of us too often believe our way is the way.
Your way may be quicker, simpler, easier.
Your way may be more traditional, more familiar.
But your way, like mine, is most likely not the only way to success.

9/2/16

One Step After Another

I want to write poems today.
I have a reading Wednesday night.
But I must read the stack of vacation snail mail.
I must read and answer some of the e-mail.
I must fill out refinance papers.
I must fill out registration papers for next week's
    conference.
I must unpack.
I must pack.
I must answer land and cell phone messages.

The list approaches ad infinitum!
But you get the picture.
And yet, I must make one step. I must act.

Thinking is good.
But all the thinking, good or bad, is just that: thinking.
To make progress, I must make a step, one step after another.

6/13/11

False Dilemma

Dilemma – two choices, one as undesirable as the other
Between the devil and the deep blue sea
Between a rock and a hard place
Between Scylla and Charybdis
Hobson's Choice
Live or die

Exaggerations!
Exaggerations all!
Neither the seriousness nor the severity may be exaggerated.
However, too often two extremes are rarely the only options.
Usually at least three options, real, ideal, and the in-between exist.
Life as it is versus life as it could be, the real versus the
      ideal—ah, the space in between!
One to infinite or at least more than two
What we don't want is consequences of either choice—and
      those, my reader, are what we so often cannot avoid!

7/4/16

A True Story

She said she was sorry.
She did.
What else could she do?
She was raped.
She was only seventeen.
Of course, she was traumatized.
Nobody doubted her.
She called the police after she passed him on the street—five
    months after the crime.
She would not know for years that the prosecutor—like many
    prosecutors—lied.
She is on a long list of women who identified the wrong man.
She could not erase the sixteen years he had spent in prison
    because she identified him as the man who raped her.
She could not replace that time—time missed with family, loved
    ones, acquaintances, strangers.
She could not erase the humiliation.
She could not rebuild his reputation.

For sixteen years he said he was innocent.
He passed two polygraph tests.
What else could he do?
How many years was he on the sexual offender list?
So, we must be grateful for the executive director who lost his
    job because the film of the story about this crime did not
    ring true for him.
He got a detective who proved the director and the accused correct.
Perhaps both the raped and innocent have a bit of peace.
Neither will have the peace they knew before the crime. Neither.

12/14/21

Health Matters

Hypertension Pill

Vitamin D

Osteoporosis pills—one morning, one night

Fish oil

Biotin

Aspirin—family health history

Gabapentin

Q-var twice a day

(Rinse mouth after each use!)

Atorvastatin

Exercises for feet

Ice feet

Splint for foot each night

CPAP machine each night

Do each of the above daily.

Sometimes she gets tired.

But then she's reminded of one or two or more whose situations
    are worse....

She always gets a burst of energy and says a prayer of gratitude.

5/5/16

My Declaration

Let my declaration be known henceforth and forever!
I will no longer let anyone take hours, a day, not to
        mention a month or years, from me.
Not again.
My time, as always, is steadily being spent.
I have not always been aware of this phenomenon.
There are people—often sincere, possibly well-meaning—
        who gobble up my time.
Attempting to be polite, I listen; I give advice.
I provide comfort.
I often sympathize, even empathize.
I give goods, money.
Shortly they return, often with the same words about the same
        problem, needing exactly what I provided earlier!
Their predicament may be worse!
They ignored my comments, explanation, suggestions.
Time was all they took.
Time is what can't be replaced.
My rant is about time.
I do not have enough of it.
I can no longer afford to squander it.
Be warned!

11/27/21

Fault Lines

Abused. Beaten. Molested. Raped.
Nobody knows all of what goes through our
        minds when we experience any of the above.
What so many of us endure is known by us only,
        be it "normal" or not.
Our fears—poverty, failure, rejection—can be
        tremendous impediments.
The fewer fears, the more freedom.
When the fears are dressed as abuse, beatings, molestation, rape,
        the victimizer may have a superficial idea, may have
        accomplished personal goals but cannot see, probably
        doesn't care to see the impact of the attack, depth of
        the pain, the degree of the trauma.
The person enduring the trauma is the only one aware of the depth
        and breadth of the pain.
Like fault lines in the earth, fault lines in people are everywhere.
Fault lines come in all sizes—small, medium, and large.
We can't always tell why the fission will take place,
        how wide or deep it will be, but worst is not knowing
        when it will be.
We can't tell the damage that will ensue.
But at least some of us know of the existence of
        fault lines.

5/4/16

Loving You PERIOD

I wish I loved you PERIOD.

I want to love you PERIOD.

But I love you BUT.

I know I do.

I can attempt to ignore the BUT but have had too many
    experiences where ignoring, regardless of effort,
    proved futile.

Loving BUT puts both you and me at a disadvantage.

Both of us spend time on the BUT—attempting to
    change it or adapt to it, alternately falsely attempting to
    convince ourselves the BUT does not matter.

However, at various times we are aware that BUT can
    destroy what is, perhaps not immediately, but eventually—
    today, tomorrow, next year, or several years away.

So now there's the BUT plus when it becomes too much.

Loving BUT can unbalance you and me.

Bold persons take a deep breath and dive in.

Or is it bold persons who say goodbye and walk away?

Granted, this can be overthinking.

All of this can be paralyzing.

Surely you can see why I wish I loved you PERIOD:

I want to love you PERIOD.

My integrity compels me to admit I love you BUT.

6/16/16

INDEX

The Absence of a Presence 19
Abstract and Concrete ....…...... 72
Acceptable? 14
An Addendum 47
Another Misunderstanding 90
Asking for Help 13
Being 44
Capital Punishment 36
A Chance? 15
Chasm 71
The Color of One's Skin 32
Complain Plus 60
Crispus Attucks 16
The Day the Pill Went on the Market 46
Degrees of Strange 49
Dollars at the Dollar Store 79
Don't Cross the Line 55
Emmett Till—Once More and Again 85
Express Yourself 59
False Dilemma 99
Fault Lines 103
The Flag and the Poor 73
Futility of Worry 34
A Gimmick 95

A Good Catch	10
Health Matters	101
A Hog Speaks: Wall Street Humans	28
Hurts	89
I Am in a Hurry!	1
Ignorance May Not Be Bliss	88
Journeys	25
The Last Look	9
Last March	75
Lies Some of Us Sometimes Tell	56
The Long Reach of the Grim Reaper	57
Loving You PERIOD	104
Minds and Marriage	35
Morning Greetings	41
Murderers	70
Musings	64
My Declaration	102
My Wants	2
Not Knowing What to Say	86
Not the One	37
Not Winning	96
On Means of Coping	87
One Step After Another	98
An Outsider Speaks	42
Pie Chart of My Life	45
Points	93
Poses of the Imposter	58
Precarity	3
Preoccupied with Horror	43
Qualify, Please Qualify	53

Randomness of the Grim Reaper	40
Reclaiming Time	26
Resiliency	38
Same Goal?	78
The Science of Listening	77
Seeing the Light	36
Speaking the Wish	82
Suspend Disbelief	92
Thank You, Mr. Trump!	5
Thanks, 63,000,000	39
That Look	48
They Do Not Know What They Do	11
Trapped in an Era	27
A Tribute to Unknown Civil Rights Workers	80
A True Story	100
Undeserved Guilt	33
Validation	74
Voices	69
Want to Judge?	21
The Washerwoman	83
Welfare	94
What Can't and Can Be Imagined	30
What They Do	18
What to Do	62
What to Take When	63
What Trump Can't Do	6
What's American—Or Not	20
Where Is He?	4
Whose America?	17
Winning Me Over	54
Your Way	97

Georgia Stewart McDade

ABOUT THE AUTHOR

Georgia Stewart McDade, a Louisiana native who has lived in Seattle more than half her life, loves reading and writing. Earning a Bachelor of Arts from Southern University, Master of Arts from Atlanta University, and Ph. D. from University of Washington, the English major spent more than thirty years teaching at Tacoma Community College as well as other institutions on various levels. As a charter member of the African-American Writers' Alliance (AAWA), McDade began reading her stories in public in 1991. For a number of years she has written poems inspired by art at such sites as Gallery 110 and Onyx Fine Arts Collective. She regularly contributed opinion pieces to Pacific Newspapers, especially the *South District Journal*, and reported for and Bellevue College radio station KBCS. Today she contributes to *South Seattle Emerald* and *Leschinews*, conducts and participates in a variety of writing workshops, and does interviews for KVRU (105.7). A prolific writer, she has works in several anthologies: six by AAWA, *Emerald Reflections*, and *WA 129*. Her works include *Travel Tips for Dream Trips*, questions and answers about her six-month, solo trip around the world; *Outside the Cave*, four volumes of poetry; and *Observations and Revelations*, a collection of stories and essays. You can hear her on Writers Read via Zoom, and sponsored by Columbia City Branch of the King County Library system each second Friday of the month. Among her several writing projects are two biographies and journals kept during her travels.

www.ingramcontent.com/pod-product-compliance
Lightning Source LLC
Chambersburg PA
CBHW070926010526
44110CB00056B/2206